Contents

Any words appearing in the text in bold, **like this**, are explained in the glossary. You can also look out for them in the Word bank at the bottom of each page.

Home sweet home

Ten to a bed!

For hundreds of years, having your own bedroom was unheard of for most young people. It was quite normal for all members of the family to share the same bedroom. Not only that, brothers and sisters often all slept together in the same bed (below)!

It is the middle of the night. You wake suddenly to find snow falling on your face. The muddy floor under your wet blankets is beginning to freeze. You try to get back to sleep, but grunts and squeals wake you again. One of the pigs in the straw beside you is giving birth. But the smell, noise, and cold are just like any other night in the rotting old hut that is home.

Perhaps this seems too grim to be someone's home. But for many people throughout history, this would have been normal. Many others would have been lucky to have any shelter at all.

Home truths

Even just 100 years ago, many people around the world had nowhere to live. Those who did often had little more than shelter from the weather . . . and sometimes not even that! Living rough on the streets was far more common than today.

Where you live and who you live with can have a big effect on your life. Your home can affect how you grow up, and who you become. It is amazing how so many people once survived at all with their dreary **dwellings** or frightful families. In fact, you might be surprised by some of the scary "home truths" that follow. . .

Sleeping rough on the streets was sometimes the only choice.

Find out later...

Why did some parents kill their children?

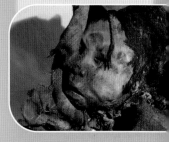

How did families manage in the days before indoor flushing toilets?

Why did some young people live with families of wolves?

Ancient times

Igloos

You might think living in an igloo – a home made of ice blocks – would be far too cold. In fact, igloos can be very cosy! The **Inuit** people from Canada (below), Alaska, and Greenland built them in the freezing winters. Their domed snow houses kept them snug and helped them survive the snowstorms.

The very first humans to walk on Earth needed places to live that would keep them safe. They had to find shelter to protect them from the weather, from enemies, and from wild animals. Long before they learned how to build shelters, many of them lived in caves.

The earliest cave dwellers are often called cavemen. They lived over 2 million years ago, during the time known as the Stone Age. Remains of their stone tools and cave wall paintings help to show us how they lived. But living in caves must have been risky – what if bears or tigers decided to move in?

Word bank   **Inuit**   native people of Alaska, Greenland, and northern Canada

Living in caves

Many groups of people choose to live inside caves. Cave **dwellings** from thousands of years ago have been found in the United States. Some were still lived in just a few hundred years ago, by some Native American tribes of Colorado, Utah, and New Mexico. Their caves and dug-out tunnels can still be seen today in places such as the Gila Cliff Dwellings National Monument in New Mexico. They show the homes of the **Mogollon** people who lived in the Gila Canyon from about 1280 to the 1300s.

The Cliff Palace is an ancient cave settlement at the Mesa Verde National Park, Colorado. It was built between AD 1190 and 1280.

People still live in these old cave dwellings in Cappadocia, Turkey.

Mogollon Native American people who lived in Arizona and New Mexico over 700 to 800 years ago

China and Egypt

When people first began to build shelters to live in, their homes were often like small caves, made of mud. The mud came from areas where rivers flooded. The fine **sediments** would set like cement when it dried out. This was just right for building walls.

China

Even as long as 4,000 years ago many Chinese families baked bricks in ovens to build their houses. The home and family was seen as very important in ancient China. Children were taught to respect their parents and obey older people without question. The oldest male was the head of the family, and everyone in the home had to do just as he said.

Whitewashed houses on the banks of the River Nile at Edfu, Egypt.

Long ago

Chinese **civilization** began around 8,000 years ago. At this time a group called the Yangshao settled near the Huang He River. Remains of some of their ancient villages have been discovered (above). In one village there are remains of farmhouses, built partly underground. They have plaster floors and roofs held up with wooden posts.

Word bank   **civilization**   way of life of a particular race of people

Egypt

Over 4,000 years ago families in ancient Egypt lived in small, brick houses near the River Nile. Whenever the river flooded, huge areas of thick, sticky mud were left behind. This mud was mixed with chopped straw and poured into moulds. These were left in the sun to dry out and bake into hard bricks.

Houses often needed to be repaired when the River Nile flooded badly and washed bricks away. Rats also chewed through the walls, so bricks often had to be patched up. Some homes were **whitewashed**, and roofs were covered with reeds topped with mud plaster.

This sculpture from about 2,410 BC shows an ancient Egyptian family with three children.

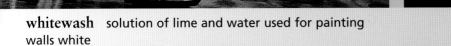
whitewash   solution of lime and water used for painting walls white

9

Romans and Greeks

Around 2,000 years ago the Romans and Greeks had very strong views about family life, how to raise children, and about teaching children right from wrong.

In Roman homes many people often lived together under one roof. This was because the **extended family** stayed together, including grandparents, aunts and uncles, and even slaves. In some rich households the slaves became treated just like family. Fathers were the bosses of the home, and they even had the right to kill their children if they did not do as they were told!

Rich and poor

As in all times and places, Roman homes were very different according to the wealth of the family. The rich lived in large palaces with many rooms and painted walls. The poor lived in tiny apartments with many people living in one room. Little has changed over thousands of years.

Roman villas were often covered with beautiful **mosaic** patterns.

Word bank   **extended family**   family of parents, children, and other relatives (grandparents, aunts, or uncles)

Spartans

If you were born in the Greek city-state of Sparta, you really belonged to the state rather than to your family. Spartans also had to grow up to be tough, because they were trained for war.

If a baby Spartan looked fit and strong, it was allowed to live. If it looked sickly, it was taken up a mountain and left to die. Babies were also washed in wine in the belief this made them strong. At the age of seven, young Spartans left home to join the army. They slept on reeds with thistles – the prickles were supposed to warm them up. No one dared to complain!

Tough living

Spartan boys were raised in camps where they were kept hungry. In this way they learned how to steal food, which was seen as good training for wartime. If a boy was caught stealing, one of the older Spartans in charge would beat him and bite the back of his hand. The boy was not being punished for stealing, but for being caught!

The 1964 movie *The 300 Spartans* shows the Spartans at their toughest.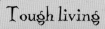

mosaic colourful patterns made from pieces of tile, glass, or stone

Aztecs and Incas

The Aztec people lived in Mexico nearly 900 years ago. When a couple married, they were given their own plot of land by the village so they could grow their own food. They could ask for more land when their children were born. A family could gain even more land if the father fought bravely in the Aztec wars. If the family failed to farm the land well, it could be taken away from them.

If a child behaved badly, he or she would be pricked with cactus spines, or made to breathe the smoke of burning chilli peppers.

Young
Aztec slaves

What would you think if your parents sold you so they could make some money? Aztec parents who could not afford to raise their children would sometimes sell a child to work for another family.

Aztec slaves struggle under the weight of their baskets. ⋮

A painting of a human sacrifice by the artist Diego Duran, from 1579. ⋯⋮

sacrifice   killing of a victim as part of a worship ceremony

Young Incas

The Inca people lived in South America, in parts of Peru and Chile, from about 1200 to 1535. They had many different gods, and believed they had to please them all the time. That could be risky for young people, who were often **sacrificed** as a peace offering. The Inca chief's children were at greatest risk as they were thought to be perfect, making them the ideal offering. Villagers walked up into the mountains where the young person was hit on the head. The victim was buried and left to die. It was hoped that this would keep the gods happy.

Proof

Frozen mummies of Inca child sacrifices have been found high in the mountains of South America (below). It is not certain if the children were freely offered by their parents, or if they were just taken from their parents against their will. The victims were covered in blankets and robes, and buried – often still alive.

Living together

Today we spend a lot of time and money trying to keep homes clean and tidy. Long ago, large families often lived in dirty rooms, but did not know about the health risks.

Dirt

About 700 years ago, in the time now called the **Middle Ages,** families in Europe lived in fear of disease and **plague.** Many **peasants** did not realise the rats and fleas living in their dirty homes were spreading disease.

Many cruck houses are still standing in the UK, although the **wattle and daub** building-style has been replaced with brick. ❖••••

Word bank   **cruck house**   old wooden-framed house
peasant   farm worker or poor person

Gross and grubby

Most peasants kept a few farm animals, which came into the house at night for safety. They were not house-trained, so homes were very smelly. Animals also brought flies into the house.

The houses would have been filthy, with no running water, no toilets, no baths, or wash basins. Soap was unheard of. People and their straw beds would have been covered with dirt, fleas, and lice. The toilet would have been a wooden bucket in the corner that everyone used. It would be emptied into the nearest river – where water was then collected for drinking!

Hard life

Peasant families cooked and slept in the same dirty room. If the cruck house was big enough, children would have slept up in a loft. Even so, sleeping so close together meant that people quickly caught diseases from each other. Many children would have died before they were even five years old.

A 1513 painting by Simon Bening called *Peasants in February*.

plague   deadly disease that spreads very quickly
thatch   straw or reeds used to cover the roof of a building

Indoor toilets

Whether families lived in castles, grand houses, or in small town houses, they all needed somewhere for eating, sleeping, and for going to the toilet. In the 1500s, a visit to the toilet could be quite a grim experience.

Chamber pots were usually kept by, or under, beds in most homes, but they had to be emptied each morning. In towns, open channels ran down the main streets and people emptied their pots into them – often by throwing the contents from a window. With more and more people living in towns 500 years ago, streets quickly became very smelly.

Many medieval houses in Europe still have the "toilet room" sticking out from the outside. ••••

Word bank   cesspit   pit for waste water or sewage
chamber pot   bowl kept in a bedroom and used as a toilet

Look out below!

Many rich people's houses had a small room that stuck out from the outside wall of their home. The toilet was inside this room. The toilet seat was a plank of wood with a hole in the middle, while the toilet itself was a hole directly above the street outside. Everything that fell through the hole landed on the ground below.

Sometimes the toilets were above a **moat**, so the waste would fall straight down into the water. Sometimes there was a long channel that ran down to a **cesspit**. Cesspits were emptied by people known as "gongfermors". How would you like that job?

"Gardez l'eau!"

You can clearly see the ground outside in this reconstruction of a medieval toilet.

Watch out!

When French people threw out the waste from their chamber pots through a window, they shouted *gardez l'eau* (pronounced gar-day low), or "watch out for the water". This may be where the English word "loo", meaning toilet, comes from.

moat   trench around a castle that is usually filled with water

Setting up home in North America

Native Americans had lived across North America for thousands of years before Europeans arrived to set up new homes. In the 1600s people first began to leave Europe to settle in the area now called New England. It was so tough for them to build homes, farm stony land, and raise their children, that many died shortly after arriving.

The settler's first homes were caves or rooms dug into the ground. With these basic homes, many of the first settlers must have wondered why they ever left their safe homeland for this tough new world. Later they made log cabins to live in.

The outdoor life

Native Americans living on the Great Plains of the west lived in **tepees** (above). Tepees were tall, cone-shaped tents made of buffalo skins. They had small openings at the top and smoke flaps, so the people inside could cook and keep a wood fire for warmth. Tepees gave good shelter from the weather, and could easily be packed up and moved.

Early pioneer homes, such as this one in Nebraska, USA, were built using blocks of earth and grass.

Word bank   **pioneer**   one of the first people to explore and settle in an area

Mobile homes

Many of the new settlers set off with their families across North America, heading west. These **pioneers** travelled across rough country in their covered wagons, which were like rickety tents on wheels. Everything the family owned was crammed inside the wagon and pulled by mules or horses over hundreds of rocky miles.

Families often had to sit squashed together in the wagon all day as it jolted along. Even when they were walking alongside, the creaking and clatter of the wheels and the clanging of pots and pans hanging from the wagon must have made life on the move noisy. The journey could also be dangerous. Sometimes a wagon wheel might break and the wagon would turn over.

Night life

The pioneers only stopped their wagons in the evening. Sometimes this was the only time young people could get out and stretch their legs. The wagons would form a big circle, and a camp fire would be lit in the middle. Lookouts were posted around the camp for fear of attacks from wild animal or Native Americans.

Camp-fires provided lots of warmth and light on a cold, dark night on the Great Plains.

tepee   cone-shaped tent made of animal skin, and used as a home by some Native Americans

19

1700s – Growing up

Around 250 years ago there were many different ideas about how to bring up children – just as there are today. Young people learned how to live with others by living with their families. As today, a family could be anything from a single adult with one child, to a large group of adults with many children of all ages, all living together under one roof.

Uncle knows best

There were hundreds of different Native American tribes living all across North America in the 1700s. Many of them had their own special customs and ways of raising their young people. If a child from the Hopi tribe misbehaved, it was often up to the mother's brother to punish the child, and teach him or her right from wrong.

A Native American family, Idaho, 1897.

Word bank   **nuclear family**   small family unit of a mother and father and their children

Heading west

As **pioneer** families spread further west through North America in the 1700s, they came across more tribes of Native Americans. Some pioneers believed the Native American ways of raising children were wrong.

Native Americans

Growing up in a Native American tribe was very different from growing up in a pioneer's **nuclear family**. Many Native American groups tended to share the child-rearing, with several adults and children living together in one **tepee**. Grandparents often looked after the younger members of the tribe. Men sometimes had more than one wife, if they could look after them also. That could mean some children had several "mothers" to look after them.

Through this way of life, most Native Americans learned how to look after each other and treat everyone as one family from an early age.

No eating

Every so often, children of the Ojibwa tribe were made to go without food for a whole day. This began when the child was about the age of four or five. It was meant to prepare young people for harsh winters when they would often have to go without food for days.

A papoose is a type of sling used to carry babies. It is also the Native American word for a small child. ⋯⋮

Bush and jungle

Many **Aboriginal people** lived in small camps across the Australian bush and desert. These **nomadic** groups had to travel far and wide to find water and food in different seasons, moving the camp as they went. Their shelters were made from whatever they could find: bark, branches, reeds, and grass.

Aboriginal children were looked after by all members of the group. As soon as boys could walk, they used spears to hunt and fish. Girls learned how to cook, and how to survive in their homes, where deadly snakes and spiders could creep in at any time.

Australian bush

In the 1700s Europeans began to settle in Australia. They did not understand the way of life of the Native Australian Aboriginal people, and often saw them as a threat. Life had always been tough for young Aboriginal people growing up in the bush, but now they were also at risk of being shot by the new settlers.

A group of Aboriginal men and children at their camp, around 1880.

South America

When explorers in the 1700s travelled to distant places and came across different peoples, there were often fierce fights. The secure family life of many jungle tribes came under threat from guns, and also from the diseases that the explorers brought with them.

One of the tribes living in the rainforests of South America was the Shuar people of Ecuador. They moved from camp to camp, around the forest. The usual family group was a man, his wives, all their daughters and unmarried sons. As soon as sons married, they went to live with their first wife's parents.

The Kayapo Indians have also lived in villages near the Amazon rainforest for centuries.

Family ornaments

The Shuar people taught their children to protect each other from enemies. By killing an enemy, they believed they would have good luck and a long life. But young people also learned another skill – how to cut off and shrink the heads of enemies (above) and hang them around the family home!

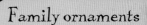

nomadic way of life with no fixed home, wandering from place to place

There have been many stories of wild children through history. One famous story tells of Romulus and Remus – twin boys who were abandoned as babies. A wolf took pity on them and raised the boys as her own, until a shepherd found them. Legend has it that Romulus went on to found the city of Rome in Italy.

Running wild

Some young people have grown up in the most frightening families. They were raised by animals in the wild!

Wild Peter

In 1724, near the German town of Hameln, a strange boy was seen running loose in the fields. People said he was a wild, black-haired creature, and they used food to catch him. The boy behaved like a trapped animal, eating raw meat and acting like a wild dog. He was taken to England and given the name Peter. He never learned to talk or laugh. However, he loved music, learned simple tasks, and could always find his way home to wherever he lived. The mysterious Peter lived until he was about 70, and died in 1785.

A 1700 painting by Charles de Lafosse shows the wolf feeding Romulus and Remus.

Word bank   **asylum**   home for those unable to care for themselves

Found in a cave

In 1767 hunters chasing a bear near Fraumark in Hungary found a teenage girl inside a bear-cave. She looked very frightened. The hunters tried to force her to leave the cave, but she did not understand them. The girl behaved like a scared, wild animal. She was very upset, but did not cry any tears. They called her "Bear Girl", and took her to the town of Karpfen.

"Bear Girl" was locked away in an **asylum** where the poor girl must have longed to be free and back in her cave. Little more is known about the girl who had grown up with a family of bears.

Was Victor, the wild boy of Aveyron, raised by a pack of wolves?

Seven-year-old Ramu, known as "Wolf Boy," was discovered living in the wild in India in 1954. Wild children are sometimes still found today.

Found in the forest

In 1799 a boy was found wandering in the woods in the south of France. He was about twelve, and could not speak. It looked as if he had lived in the wild for some time. He became known as Victor, the wild boy of Aveyron. He was taken to Paris where he died years later, aged about forty.

1800s – Hard times

Danger

During wars, some soldiers had to live near the battlefields with their wives and children (below). It was neither safe nor pleasant for them to be living in such places. They had to survive with hardly any food, water, or medicines, and were at constant risk from enemy-attack and stray bullets.

Every century had its difficult times when home life and "happy families" were at risk or in real danger. The 1800s had its fair share of hard times and **conflict**.

War

In times of war, it was not just soldiers who were in danger. Families could also be on the front line – especially in a **civil war,** where the enemy could be anywhere.

The American Civil War started in 1861. The North and the South of America disagreed about how to run the country. After four violent years, the Union States of the North beat the Confederate States of the South. Around 600,000 soldiers were killed, and their families fell into great hardship.

Word bank   **civil war** when soldiers from the same country fight against each other

Misery

Young people were hit hard by the Civil War. About 100,000 soldiers were aged only fifteen, or even younger. They had to leave home and live in terrible conditions. Many did not see their families for years. Young people helped to look after wounded soldiers, and some even served as spies.

Girls, some as young as eleven, worked as nurses. They, too, had to live and work in dismal places. Others stayed at home and made blankets for the soldiers. The war left many homes without fathers to earn money for their families. Instead, young boys had to go out to work and earn money for the family.

Scarlett O'Hara defends herself against a Union soldier in *Gone With the Wind*.

Howard Pyle's painting, *The Battle of Nashville*, shows the horrific scenes of devastation at Nashville, Tennessee, in 1864.

Enemy at the door

Union soldiers from the North were fighting to stop slavery. Many of the richer homes in the Confederate South had slaves. Union soldiers would sometimes break into homes in the South to free their slaves, or to steal the family's property (above). Families lived in fear of the enemy breaking into their home at night.

Bad housing

In the 1800s, industry grew across the United Kingdom, United States, Canada, and Australia. Huge numbers of people **migrated** to the countryside to work in the mills, mines, and workshops in the cities. But they could not all be housed properly. Many families had to crowd together in run-down **slums**. There was no running water or flushing toilets, and none of the houses had gas or electricity. Instead, there were rats, cockroaches, and often mouldy walls or rising damp. Life for millions of young people was not just dreary, it was sometimes totally miserable.

Unsafe

Many towns of the 1800s were full of chimneys belching black smoke. Poor housing and dark, smoky alleys (above) led to a growth in city crime. Criminals could easily hide and pounce on their victims. Many poor families had to live in the middle of such crime, and some even turned to stealing as a way out of their **poverty**.

Big families such as this would often have to live in one room. ••••

slum　city area of dirty run-down housing, and poor living conditions

Bad health

City slums of the 1800s were far from healthy places. People did not know that killer diseases, such as **cholera** and **typhoid**, were carried by dirty water, **infected** food, and ill people.

The streets were full of human waste and manure from the thousands of horses used at the time. In the summer heat, flies swarmed in the air, crawled over food, and spread disease throughout the slums.

In many cities the drains that were built to take away rainwater often carried raw **sewage** into rivers. These same rivers were used by thousands of families for washing and drinking. No wonder life in the slums was grim.

Moving on

At the end of the 1800s many cities began to build new and better housing for poor families. Slum clearance schemes rehoused many people. Rows of cheap **terraced** housing or high-rise **tenements** were built. Many of these became the slums of the 1900s.

Children play in the slum tenements of Chicago in the late 1800s.

tenement   separate residence within a house or block of flats

29

Manhattan

The English writer Charles Dickens wrote a lot about dreary **dwellings** and frightful families. In 1842 he toured Five Points. This was a **slum** area in lower Manhattan, New York. He said it was full of filth and worse than many of the slums he had seen in the United Kingdom. He said: "all that is **loathsome**, drooping, and decayed is here."

New York

Towards the end of the 1800s, large cities in the United States had more problems than ever before. Many people from all over the world **migrated** to these cities in the hope of finding work and starting new lives.

For many new **immigrants**, New York was seen as the best place to set up home. They soon discovered that damp, dirty, dark, and crumbling buildings were all they could find to live in. With so many different groups of people living side by side in cramped housing, gang warfare and violence erupted on the streets.

An immigrant family living in poor conditions in the slums of New York. ⋯⋗

Word bank

abbatoir   place where animals are killed for food
immigrant   someone who moves to another country to stay

Hell's Kitchen

One of the most violent places to live in New York was called Hell's Kitchen. In the **Civil War** in the 1860s, over 350,000 people crowded into Hell's Kitchen. They were squeezed into rows of **tenements** in the middle of the **abattoirs** and factories. The area had such a terrible smell of dead animals that 39th Street was nicknamed "Abattoir Place". Just the place for young people to grow up!

Two small girls rummage through trash looking for food, New York, early 1900s.

Living on the streets

In the late 1860s thousands of children who had been **orphaned** in the Civil War ended up living rough on the streets of New York. They became homeless street **urchins** who slept in back alleys and brick yards. Many of them became criminals and members of violent gangs.

orphan   child whose parents are dead
urchin   mischievous child, especially raggedly dressed

Poorhouse rules

Orange County New York 1831

"At meal times when the bell is rung, all who are able to attend shall eat together. No one shall speak or whisper at the table, or else they will be removed and **deprived** of that meal. Anyone who is late shall go without that meal, unless there are good reasons."

Homes for the poor

However bad some homes were, they were probably better than no home at all. In the days when there was no **welfare state**, what became of **orphans** or children thrown out of their homes by cruel parents?

Often the Church helped to look after homeless young people, but in the 1800s there were often too many of them in the world's towns and cities. Homeless children, and sometimes whole families, ended up living in **workhouses** in the United Kingdom.

Men queue for dinner at the Blackwells Island poorhouse, in New York, in this 1875 drawing. ⋯⋗

Word bank   deprived   kept from having something important

Dreadful dwellings

In a workhouse, people of all ages slept in crowded rooms in cold, dark buildings, and ate nothing but **gruel** every day. Everyone worked hard for long hours, and family members were usually kept apart. Many workhouses were run like this, with very strict rules. This was the only home that many poor people knew.

In the 1800s the United States ran poorhouses where needy people lived together, with many strict rules. It was not until 1875 that laws were made to stop children being brought up in such grim places.

Find out what happened to Jackie Coogan, the child star in this Chaplin movie on page 40...

Rags to riches

In 1896 a seven-year-old British boy, called Charlie Chaplin, was sent to live in a London workhouse because his mother was too ill and poor to look after him. When he grew up, he moved to Hollywood, United States, and became the highest paid movie star of the 1920s.

welfare state system where the government provides basic levels of living for the poor

1900s – On the move

Did you know?

In the 1800s in Ireland, the potato crops kept failing. We now know this time as the **Irish potato famine**. Thousands of people had to leave their homes or risk **starvation**. Many travelled to other countries to find food and work. Some became full-time travellers, carrying on this way of life throughout the 1900s.

Having a place to call home can give people a sense of belonging. In the 1900s moving home was far less common than it is now. Many people stayed in the same house for life. People did not change jobs much at all – transport was so limited that people had to live near to where they worked.

Life on the road

Some people have never left home – as they take it with them wherever they go! For hundreds of years travellers have set up camp by the roadside as they journey from place to place.

Irish **immigrants** wait at Ellis Island, hoping to be allowed into the United States.

Word bank   **abode**   place where someone stays or lives

Travellers

For many families it is their chosen way of life to uproot their home from time to time and move on. They may keep moving to find different work in different seasons, or they just prefer life on the open road with "no fixed **abode**".

Some people, like this family in 1905, prefer a life of travelling to staying in one place.

Little and large members of a travelling circus, 1922.

Homes on wheels

Some people like the idea of mobile homes so much that they spend holidays camping in tents or caravans. But could you live "on the move" all the time and in all weathers? Some people had no choice – if they worked in circuses or funfairs. Their children grew up on the move, travelling to different towns and countries.

starvation   die from hunger

Orphan trains

Many young people in the late 1800s and early 1900s had to grow up without their own parents and in places they did not know.

Between 1854 and 1929, as many as 250,000 children from New York and other US cities were sent by train to new homes. The homes were in towns in the west of the United States, and Canada and Mexico. The government thought some young people would have a better life in these new homes.

The trains were called **"orphan** trains", but few of the young people were really orphans. Many just could not find work, and their parents could not afford to keep them at home.

WANTED

HOMES FOR CHILDREN

A company of homeless children from the East will arrive at

Troy, Missouri, on 25 February, 1910.

These children have been thrown friendless upon the world. They come from the Children's Aid Society of New York. Citizens of this community are asked to give them good homes. They must treat them in every way as a member of the family.

New homes

The orphan trains steamed their way west, with the young people on board not knowing where they would end up, or who would look after them. As the train made its stops, everyone had to get out and line up in front of a crowd of onlookers. Many people wanted to give a home to an "orphan", but some just needed another worker on their farm. Many young people were taken and used as cheap **labour**. Brothers and sisters were often split up, and they lost all contact with their family.

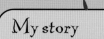
My story

"In 1925 my brother Fred and I were removed from our home in New York because of **neglect**. I was three and my brother was six. We were put on a train with other children and sent to Nebraska. We were separated and went to different foster homes. Luckily they were good homes. Many years later we were finally reunited."

–Howard Hurd,
who died in 2002.

A group of "orphans" wait to be sent on the "orphan trains" in 1918. Who knows what became of them?

Many brothers and sisters were split up from each other in the early 1900s.

neglect   leave uncared for

World War 2

World War 2 was the first time that ordinary homes and families became the targets of enemy bombs. German bombs began to fall on European cities in 1940, and millions of homes were destroyed.

Hundreds of thousands of young people were **evacuated** to safer places in the countryside. Some of the homes were dismal, and some **evacuees** were treated badly by the people looking after them. Other homes were far grander than their own homes in the cities. Some young people were sent to the United States, Canada, and Australia, and never returned home.

Memories

"Three children came to stay with us. We got on well until one of the evacuees picked all the heads off the flowers in the garden and blamed me. My mother beat me, but she later realised I had told the truth all along. We often heard the evacuees sobbing in their beds at night."

– A woman from Worcester, UK, who grew up in the 1940s, and whose family took in war evacuees.

Young children carry their suitcases as they are evacuated in 1940.

Word bank   evacuate   remove people from a place of danger

Worrying times

When Japanese planes bombed the US naval base at Pearl Harbor in 1941, people became worried that US homes would be attacked next. In fact, Americans remained safe at home. But family life became difficult, with many parents away fighting the war. Shops ran out of goods, as the ships bringing them into the country were attacked by German submarines.

The attack on Pearl Harbor in 1941 destroyed many buildings and killed many US people.

Living in secret

During the **Holocaust** in World War 2 some people had to hide in their homes. It was unsafe to make a noise indoors, let alone go outside. For two years, Anne Frank and her family hid from German soldiers in a small attic in Amsterdam, the Netherlands. They were found in 1944 and sent to concentration camps where Anne died just before the war ended. Her diary was published in 1947.

Anne Frank writing her famous diary in the secret attic.

More home truths

Scariest family

The Addams Family was a television show in the 1960s. This weird family lived in a spooky house that terrified all visitors. Uncle Fester had staring eyes and a mouth that lit up light bulbs. The actor who played Fester was Jackie Coogan, who first played an **orphan** in *The Kid* with Charlie Chaplin in 1921 (see page 33).

We love taking a peek inside some of the strange homes and scary places where people live. Many of today's television programmes try to show how "ordinary" people live. Some people just want to watch how other families spend their time, decorate their houses, or cope with "neighbours from hell". We like to see how other people live together, what their homes are like, and what happens behind closed doors. **Dwellings** and families have become a huge part of today's popular entertainment.

This strange house-boat, was built in California in 1993.

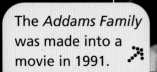

The *Addams Family* was made into a movie in 1991.

Weird homes

So many modern houses on large housing estates look alike, so it is hardly surprising that some people want to make their homes look different. The strange buildings some people live in can make popular television viewing. One television series called *America's Weirdest Homes* travels around the United States, filming the most unusual and bizarre homes. It seems some people will do anything not to have dreary dwellings today!

Who would live in a house like this?

A nursery rhyme told of an old woman who had so many children that she sent them all to bed . . . in a shoe. Strange as it seems, people can, and do, live in a shoe! So why did Mahlon Haines build his famous Shoe House in Hellam, Pennsylvania in 1948 (above)? To advertise his shoe stores, of course.

No place like home

Many young people today have to deal with homelessness, which is still a major problem all around the world. The facts are shocking:

- Around 150 million children are living on their own in streets around the world.
- At least 1 billion people live in **slums** today, mostly in Asia, Africa, and South America.
- By 2050, there may be 2.5 billion people in the world living in slums.

HAPPY FAMILIES
(2003)

A UK couple has made it into the Guinness Book of Records for having the world's longest marriage. Percy and Florence Arrowsmith, aged 105 and 100 years old, have been married for 80 years. They have three children, six grandchildren, and nine great-grandchildren. Mrs Arrowsmith said, "The most important thing is that we still love one another."

Sadly, Percy died soon after this story was released.

A slum in Mumbai (Bombay), India. The rich area of Mumbai is in the background. ⋯⟶

Homeless

Many homeless young people today live wherever they can find shelter from the weather and a space to sleep. They use candles for light, worn rugs to keep warm, and rubbish to burn for cooking meals. In Mongolia's freezing cities, where the temperature can drop to −35 °C (−31 °F), the sewers are the warmest place for street kids. Richer countries also have their share of families in crisis. The lack of **affordable** housing still leaves many people homeless, even in the richest cities of the world.

Despite their grim homes, many people still think that who they live with is what really matters. After all, living with those you love and trust is still one of the most important things about the place you call home.

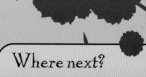

Where next?

Looking back at all the different types of homes and the people that lived in them through history, perhaps you appreciate your own home even more! With so many people still living in terrible conditions, the challenge facing all of us now is to make homelessness a thing of the past.

Teenagers serve Christmas dinner at a homeless shelter in Minnesota, US.

Find out more

Little beggars

In the 1700s, London had a big problem with child beggars, with no home or family...

14 February, 1734

A great number of loose idle vagabonds, street-walkers, women with wheel-barrows, carrying dice to cheat children and servants, who infest the streets of this city, have been lately committed to Bridewell prison.

– Grub-Street Journal

Further reading

A *Plains Indian Village*, Stuart A. Kallen and P. M. Boekhoff (Kidhaven, 2002)

Medieval Life, Andrew Langley (DK Eyewitness Books, 2002)

The Real Hannah Green: An Orphan Train Story, Kathleen M. Muldoon (Perfection Learning, 2003)

Using the Internet

Explore the Internet to find out more about childhood homes through the ages. You can use a search engine, such as **www.yahooligans.com**, and type in keywords such as:

- Anne Frank
- pioneers
- workhouse

Search tips

There are billions of pages on the Internet so it can be difficult to find exactly what you are looking for.

These search tips will help you find useful websites more quickly:

- Know exactly what you want to find out about first.
- Use two to six keywords in a search, putting the most important words first.
- Be precise. Only use names of people, places, or things.

Big families!

A kibbutz is a group of people living together, sharing everything. Adults and children do not live in separate families. Children are brought up by everyone. The first kibbutz was started in Deganya in Palestine in 1909, in what is now Israel.

Family records

According to the *Guinness World Records* in 2001, the highest recorded number of children born to one mother is 69! Between 1725 and 1765, a woman in Shuya, Russia gave birth to sixteen pairs of twins, seven sets of triplets, and four sets of quadruplets. 67 of them survived and grew up.

King-size family

In 2005 the Samantas family all lived together in one big house in Kolkata, India. 93 people from four generations lived under one roof, sharing the same kitchen. The eldest was 97-year-old Sonamoni. The youngest was her 4-month-old great-grandson, Rikky. Quite a family!

Latchkey children

A " latchkey child" is a child who lets themselves in, or who stays on their own at home for part of the day, whilst their parents are still at work. The term "latchkey child" actually started in the early 1800s, when the young people who had to look after themselves wore the key to their home tied on a string around their necks.

Glossary

abbatoir place where animals are killed for food

abode place where someone stays or lives

Aboriginal people native people of Australia

affordable able to be bought and paid for

asylum home for those unable to care for themselves

cesspit pit for waste water or sewage

chamber pot bowl kept in a bedroom and used as a toilet

cholera deadly disease with severe vomiting and diarrhoea

civilization way of life of a particular race of people

civil war when soldiers from the same country fight against each other

conflict sharp disagreement or fight

cruck house old wooden-framed house

deprived kept from having something important

dwelling place where people live

evacuate remove people from a place of danger

evacuee person who has been sent away from a place of danger

extended family family of parents, children, and other relatives (grandparents, aunts, or uncles)

garderobe toilet holes in the outer walls of buildings, which often dropped into cesspits

gruel watery soup made from mashed oats

Holocaust the killing of millions of Jews by the German Nazi Government during World War 2

immigrant someone who moves to another country to stay

infected be affected by disease or unfit for use

Inuit native people of Alaska, Greenland, and northern Canada

Irish potato famine widespread famine in Ireland between 1845 and 1851 when the potato crops failed

labour work done for payment

loathsome very unpleasant

Middle Ages period of European history from about AD 500–1500

migrate movement of people from one country to another

moat trench around a castle that is usually filled with water

Mogollon Native American people who lived in Arizona and New Mexico over 700 to 800 years ago

mosaic colourful patterns made from pieces of tile, glass, or stone

neglect leave uncared for

nomadic way of life with no fixed home, wandering from place to place

nuclear family small family unit of a mother and father and their children

orphan child whose parents are dead

peasant farm worker or poor person

pioneer one of the first people to explore and settle in an area

plague deadly disease that spreads very quickly

poverty being extremely poor

sacrifice killing of a victim as part of a worship ceremony

sediment matter carried by water or wind and deposited on the seabed

sewage waste materials carried off by sewers

slum city area of dirty run-down housing, and poor living conditions

starvation die from hunger

tenement separate residence within a house or block of flats

tepee cone-shaped tent made of animal skins, and used as a home by some Native Americans

terrace row of houses built in one block in a uniform style

thatch straw or reeds used to cover the roof of a building

typhoid fever caused by bacteria in dirty food or water

urchin mischievous child, especially raggedly dressed

wattle and daub building material of twigs, plastered with mud or clay

welfare state system where the government provides basic levels of living for the poor

whitewash solution of lime and water used for painting walls white

workhouse institution in the United Kingdom where the poor were given a place to live in return for their hard work

Index